The Promise
of Security

BETH MOORE

The Promise of Security

Tyndale House Publishers, Inc.
Carol Stream, Illinois

Visit Tyndale's exciting Web site at www.tyndale.com.

Visit Beth Moore's Web site at www.lproof.org and this book's Web site at www.solonginsecurity.com.

TYNDALE and Tyndale's quill logo are registered trademarks of Tyndale House Publishers, Inc.

The Promise of Security

Published in association with Yates & Yates (www.yates2.com).

Unless otherwise indicated, all Scripture quotations are taken from the *Holy Bible*, New Living Translation, copyright © 1996, 2004, 2007 by Tyndale House Foundation. Used by permission of Tyndale House Publishers, Inc., Carol Stream, Illinois 60188. All rights reserved.

Scripture quotations marked NIV are taken from the *Holy Bible*, New International Version®, NIV®. Copyright © 1973, 1978, 1984 by Biblica, Inc.™ Used by permission of Zondervan. All rights reserved worldwide.

ISBN 978-1-4143-3796-8

Printed in the United States of America

16   15   14   13   12   11
8   7   6

Contents

When life seems unpredictable and uncertain . . .

Jesus Christ is the same yesterday, today, and forever.   HEBREWS 13:8

WE TAKE OUR first breath of terrestrial air in total shock. Christ alone is unchanged and will remain unchanged for all of eternity.

We, on the other hand, are in constant, hair-raising, stomach-turning flux. As the old saying goes, nothing stays the same but change.

The truth is, God uses change to change *us*. He doesn't use it to destroy us or to distract us but to coax us to the next level of character, experience, compassion, and destiny.

• • •

What sorrow awaits you who build big houses with money gained dishonestly! You believe your wealth will buy security, putting your family's nest beyond the reach of danger.   HABAKKUK 2:9

THOUSANDS OF YEARS ago, an old prophet spoke these words that are frighteningly consistent with many of the headlines we're seeing on news magazines during this nation's current economic crisis.

No amount of wealth can buy security. Every rich man and woman in the world is squirming in that reality right now. You and I have learned along the way that our need is far deeper than our circumstances and more cavernous than our pockets can plunge. Our world system has made financial promises it can't keep, and though its confessions are made only in whispers, if we'll listen closely, it's finally admitting the lie.

• • •

When I was prosperous, I said, "Nothing
can stop me now!" Your favor, O LORD,
made me secure as a mountain. Then you
turned away from me, and I was shattered.

PSALM 30:6-7

JUST WHEN I'M feeling all secure, like I'm God's best friend, an earthquake splits that lofty mountain right down the middle. And boy, am I dismayed. I have a feeling we can never get so secure in ourselves that we cannot be moved. Can a rock ever move forward?

Maybe I just get bored easily. I'm forever wanting to go someplace with God. I forget that in order to really want to *go*, something has to happen to make me want to leave where I am. Maybe we're all just sick to death of taking three steps forward and two steps back. Call me a math wizard, but isn't that still one step forward? Isn't that still some pretty big progress as we run against the hurricane winds of a godless culture? And if we don't lose that ground, aren't we on our way somewhere new? Willing to take three more steps—even if we lose two?

• • •

*I am certain that God, who began the good
work within you, will continue his work
until it is finally finished on the day when
Christ Jesus returns.*

PHILIPPIANS 1:6

I HATE TO display such a firm grasp of the obvious, but how will we ever change if everything
around us stays the same? Or what will ever cause
us to move on to the next place He has for us
if something doesn't happen to change the way
we feel about where we are? God is thoroughly
committed to finishing the masterpiece He started
in us. And that process means one major thing:
change.

• • •

*What we suffer now is nothing compared to
the glory he will reveal to us later.*

ROMANS 8:18

THE FUTURE WE have coming is so glorious that
nothing we've suffered will compare to the mag-
nitude and splendor of it. We must not let the

enemy of our souls get away with convincing us that anything can utterly destroy us. If we do, we will hand him an engraved invitation to attend our constant torment.

Over and over Jesus implores His followers, "Take courage!" as if His hand is outstretched and His palm opened with offered treasure. It's time we took Him up on it. Do we really want to spend our time rehearsing deaths of all kinds rather than engaging in the effervescence of life?

• • •

When you long to be healthy and whole . . .

> *The temptations in your life are no different from what others experience. And God is faithful. He will not allow the temptation to be more than you can stand. When you are tempted, he will show you a way out so that you can endure.*
>
> 1 CORINTHIANS 10:13

BY THE GRACE and power of God, I've had the exhilarating joy of winning many battles, some of them against no small foes. But I have not won this particular battle against the stronghold of insecurity. *Yet.*

God help me, I'm going to. This one's too deeply woven into the fabric of my female soul

to deal with amid a bagful of other strongholds.
Thank God, a time comes in a willing life when
you're ready to face a Goliath-sized foe all by itself
and fight it to the stinking death.

• • •

You are not controlled by your sinful nature.
You are controlled by the Spirit if you have
the Spirit of God living in you. (And remem-
ber that those who do not have the Spirit of
Christ living in them do not belong to him
at all.)   ROMANS 8:9

ALTHOUGH WE MAY have something unhealthy
deep inside of us, those in whom Christ dwells
also have something deeper. Something whole.
Something so infinitely healthy that, if it would
but invade the rest of us, we would be healed.

I am so thankful that at no time since I received
Christ as Savior have I ever been a total wreck.
Partial? Lord, have mercy, yes. Humiliatingly so.
But total? Not on your ever-loving life. And if He
resides in you, neither have you.

• • •

May the Lord our God show us his approval and make our efforts successful. Yes, make our efforts successful! PSALM 90:17

JESUS IS NOT unhealthy. Not codependent with us. His strength is made perfect in our weakness. This thought never grows old to me: He has no dark side. In Him is *no darkness at all.*

That, beloved, is our challenge. To let the healthy, utterly whole, and completely secure part of us increasingly overtake our earthen vessels until it drives our every emotion, reaction, and relationship. When we allow God's truth to eclipse every false positive and let our eyes spring open to the treasure we *have*, there in His glorious reflection we'll also see the treasure we *are*. And the beauty of the Lord our God will be upon us.

• • •

When you lack confidence . . .

*I don't consider myself inferior in any way
to these "super apostles" who teach such
things. I may be unskilled as a speaker,
but I'm not lacking in knowledge. We have
made this clear to you in every possible way.*

2 CORINTHIANS 11:5-6

I LOVE THE apostle Paul. Honestly, he's one of my
favorite people in the entire stretch of Scripture,
but maybe one reason he appeals to me so much is
because he was enormously used of God *in spite of
himself.* Don't think for a moment he didn't fight his
own flesh just like the rest of us. Take, for instance,
the way he felt the need to affirm his credentials to
the people he served in Corinth by using this little
twist described in the verse above.

The beauty of Paul wasn't his superhumanity but his unwillingness to let his weaknesses, feelings, and fears override his faith. Like us, the fiercest enemy he had to fight in the fulfillment of his destiny was himself.

• • •

Do not throw away this confident trust in the Lord. Remember the great reward it brings you! Patient endurance is what you need now, so that you will continue to do God's will. Then you will receive all that he has promised. HEBREWS 10:35-36

FLEE FROM ARROGANCE, but whatever you do, hold tightly to the confidence you have in Christ.

The enemy of your soul will never have to worry about what kind of damage you could do to the kingdom of darkness if he can get you to buy the lie that you are incompetent, weak, and inadequate. But you're not. You may be "struck down, but [you are] not destroyed" (2 Corinthians 4:9, NIV).

• • •

Whatever I am now, it is all because God poured out his special favor on me—and not without results. For I have worked harder than any of the other apostles; yet it was not I but God who was working through me by his grace.

1 CORINTHIANS 15:10

To PAUL, THE essence of the crucified life was daily dying to the part of himself that would deny, destroy, or distract from the great work of God in him. The great work of God *through* him. After untold wars with his own inner man, Paul watched as his wounded ego was wrestled to the ground by the Spirit of Christ, and up stood a person he had no inkling he could be. A stranger, you might say, to the man he'd mirrored for so long.

And his mission was accomplished.

• • •

When you feel alone . . .

> *In times of trouble, may the LORD answer*
> *your cry. May the name of the God of Jacob*
> *keep you safe from all harm.*
>
> PSALM 20:1

THE FACT THAT the inspiration of the Holy Spirit
on the pages of Scripture is not dampened by the
insecurities of those God chose to pen it is perhaps
the greatest testimony to its incomparable potency.
After the likes of Adam, Eve, Abraham, Sarah, Hagar,
Leah, Rachel, Saul, the woman at the well, the "super
apostles," and Paul, surely we can breathe a sigh of
relief that we are not alone in our struggles.

Human flesh and blood have no weakness so
strong that God's strength is made weak. He's got

what we need. It's up to us whether or not we're going to let the worst of us get the best of us.

• • •

Jesus and the ones he makes holy have the same Father. That is why Jesus is not ashamed to call them his brothers and sisters.　　HEBREWS 2:11

GOD KNOWS WE'RE insecure. But we do not need to be. And He will not leave well enough alone. He has enough security for both of us, and for those of us who call Christ Savior, He slipped His own secure Spirit within our simple jars of clay. It is in you to be secure, dear one. Do you hear what I'm saying to you? You have it in you.

• • •

When you are looking for love . . .

I will be your God throughout your life-
time—until your hair is white with age.
I made you, and I will care for you. I will
carry you along and save you.

ISAIAH 46:4

EVERY ADULT STILL has a need to be loved like a child. That's why losing both parents is often a profound life transition—no matter how old you are when it happens. Just wait and see. I get that orphaned feeling every time I kneel at my parents' graves. But here's the good news: you can indeed look for that kind of love from God, and He will always love you and take care of you like the perfect father does his child.

If you've lived your life looking for someone to take care of you but you always end up taking care of everyone else, your search is over. God has what you need, and you'll never wear Him out.

• • •

The LORD is like a father to his children, tender and compassionate to those who fear him. For he knows how weak we are; he remembers we are only dust.

PSALM 103:13-14

WHAT MIGHT SURPRISE you is to know that God delights in being able to say, "Look, look, everybody! This is My child!" Yep. Even after all the foolishness.

The writer of this passage, David, was a veritable emotional volcano constantly threatening to erupt *and* a man after God's own heart.

• • •

I have chosen you and will not throw you away. Don't be afraid, for I am with you. Don't be discouraged, for I am your God.

I will strengthen you and help you. I will
hold you up with my victorious right hand.

ISAIAH 41:9-10

IF YOU'VE SUFFERED a serious case of insecurity, you
need to make sure that you're letting God tend to
it. Putting up a front doesn't work. That neon light
has a way of burning through every cover we throw
on it. God knows exactly what happened and what
a toll it took. He knows the number it played on
your mind. Let Him bring you peace. Let Him
tell you you're worth *wanting, loving, even liking,
pursuing, fighting for,* and, yes, beloved, *keeping.*

Whatever you do, don't reject the only One
wholly incapable of rejecting you.

• • •

When you are searching for significance and value . . .

*O LORD, you have examined my heart
and know everything about me. You know
when I sit down or stand up. You know my
thoughts even when I'm far away. You see
me when I travel and when I rest at home.
You know everything I do. You know what
I am going to say even before I say it, LORD.
You go before me and follow me. You place
your hand of blessing on my head. Such
knowledge is too wonderful for me, too great
for me to understand! . . . You made all the
delicate, inner parts of my body and knit
me together in my mother's womb. Thank
you for making me so wonderfully complex!*

*Your workmanship is marvelous—how well
I know it. You watched me as I was being
formed in utter seclusion, as I was woven
together in the dark of the womb. You saw
me before I was born. Every day of my life
was recorded in your book. Every moment
was laid out before a single day had passed.
How precious are your thoughts about me,
O God. They cannot be numbered!*

PSALM 139:1-6, 13-17

WE'RE ALL DESPERATE for significance. We live our lives screaming, "Somebody notice me!" And do you want to hear something interesting? That's exactly how God made us. That very need is built into our human hard drive to send us on a search for our Creator, who can assign us more significance than we can handle. He not only notices us, He never takes His eyes off of us.

Every now and then a moment of clarity hits us, and we feel *known* by something—*Someone*—of inestimable greatness.

• • •

*God has made everything beautiful for its
own time. He has planted eternity in the
human heart, but even so, people cannot see
the whole scope of God's work from begin-
ning to end.*　ECCLESIASTES 3:11

HUMILITY IS A crucial component in true security.
It's the very thing that calms the savage beast of
pride. More important, humility is the heart of the
great paradox: we find our lives when we lose them
to something much larger. Perhaps the writer of
Ecclesiastes had a hint of this in mind when he
wrote these words.

• • •

*Who can find a virtuous and capable wife?
She is more precious than rubies.*

PROVERBS 31:10

I WHOLEHEARTEDLY WANT to be a virtuous woman
and possess noble character, but in reality, the
Hebrew term used in this verse is actually most
often used to convey "valor."

I don't know what kind of courage it took

thousands of years ago, but I know how courageous women need to be today. Even in the context
of this woman's rich role in the family, can't the
home be a fierce battlefield too?

• • •

When you need strength and dignity . . .

> *Clothe yourself with the presence of the Lord*
> *Jesus Christ. And don't let yourself think*
> *about ways to indulge your evil desires.*
>
> ROMANS 13:14

WE ARE ALL probably familiar with the process of standing in front of the closet, mulling over what to wear, and then changing two or three times before we head to work or church.

When Scripture tells us to "put off your old self . . . and to put on the new self," it's inviting us to think in terms of taking off and putting on clothing (Ephesians 4:22, 24, NIV).

There is nothing weak about God. Pure, unadulterated power resting on our very shoulders.

• • •

What shall we say about such wonderful
things as these? If God is for us, who can
ever be against us?   ROMANS 8:31

THIS IS THE very moment we must head straight
to the throne of an all-powerful God and Father,
rehearsing over and over who He says we are and
what He says we're worth. We must call on Him to
fight our battles for us and through us and to stand
us on steady feet in a confidence only He can sup-
ply. We must ask Him to bring forth the women
in us that we didn't even know we were.

• • •

Her husband is well known at the city gates,
where he sits with the other civic leaders.

PROVERBS 31:23

THE FACT THAT this woman's husband was well
known at the city gave—some translations say
"respected at the city gate"—wasn't in spite of the
fact that his wife was clothed in strength and dignity, but at least in part because of it.

Pride is dignity's counterfeit. Never lose sight

of that. We don't forfeit our humility in order to get over insecurity.

• • •

When I look at the night sky and see the work of your fingers—the moon and the stars you set in place—what are mere mortals that you should think about them, human beings that you should care for them? Yet you made them only a little lower than God and crowned them with glory and honor.   PSALM 8:3-5

WHAT EXACTLY *IS* dignity? The same Hebrew term translated *dignity* in the Proverbs 31 passage about the woman of valor's apparel is found in sublime words written by the psalmist to his Creator. In the passage above, the word is translated *honor* in English instead of *dignity*, but it is derived from the same Hebrew term and holds the identical meaning. Revel in the context.

• • •

> *We are confident that he hears us whenever*
> *we ask for anything that pleases him. And*
> *since we know he hears us when we make our*
> *requests, we also know that he will give us*
> *what we ask for.*   1 JOHN 5:14-15

GOD DIDN'T JUST confer dignity to us. He *crowned* us with it. We are wise to note that all people have God-given dignity even if they don't yet have eternal life through Jesus Christ.

Hear this at a yell: it is God's will for you to have your dignity and security restored. You don't need to wrestle with this one. You don't need to read six more books. You don't need to ponder the subject matter until your next big disaster. This one is cut and dry. Neither God nor you have anything to gain by your persistent insecurity.

• • •

When your relationships need a boost . . .

When they arrived in Bethsaida, some people brought a blind man to Jesus, and they begged him to touch the man and heal him. Jesus took the blind man by the hand and led him out of the village. Then, spitting on the man's eyes, he laid his hands on him and asked, "Can you see anything now?" The man looked around. "Yes," he said. "I see people, but I can't see them very clearly. They look like trees walking around." Then Jesus placed his hands on the man's eyes again, and his eyes were opened. His sight was completely restored, and he could see everything clearly. MARK 8:22-25

THE FIRST RESULT of the encounter between Jesus and the blind man represents exactly what can happen to us on an emotional level. We can see people "like trees walking around." Not as fellow human beings. Not as peers on planet Earth. Our female eyes have a strange way of viewing the opposite sex as something more or vastly less than they really are. Nothing would do us more good right this moment than to realize that our vision is impaired and it doesn't have to stay that way.

• • •

You, O LORD, are a shield around me; you are my glory, the one who holds my head high. PSALM 3:3

LET'S PRAY FOR our husbands, sons, brothers, nephews, friends, and fathers. Thank God for each one of them by name, and ask Him to make them courageous and mighty in His strength in their spheres of influence. Ask Him to be a shield around them, to be their glory and the lifter of their heads.

• • •

*God knows that your eyes will be opened as
soon as you eat it, and you will be like God,
knowing both good and evil.*

GENESIS 3:5

THERE YOU HAVE it. The first human pursuit of
omniscience.

Do you remember the story? The serpent
used powerfully shrewd and deceptive reasoning
to tempt the woman to disregard divine instruc-
tion and eat from the one forbidden tree. And
Eve wanted to know what only God was meant
to know.

I'm not a proponent of ignorance or denial.
The pursuit of knowledge for the edification of
soul and community is a priority passion. But Eve
went where she did not belong and acquired what
she could not confront. She already knew in her
heart what she needed to know. When she insisted
on a little slice of omniscience (knowing what God
alone needed to know), she ended up with infor-
mation she could not handle.

• • •

> *I want you to know how much I have*
> *agonized . . . for many other believers who*
> *have never met me personally. I want them*
> *to be encouraged and knit together by strong*
> *ties of love. I want them to have complete*
> *confidence that they understand God's*
> *mysterious plan, which is Christ himself. In*
> *him lie hidden all the treasures of wisdom*
> *and knowledge.* COLOSSIANS 2:1-3

TELL GOD WHAT keeps haunting you. Ask Him to grant you His own words to recite the moment you replay those old conversations and images. Then take all that insatiable desire to delve into the unknown and focus it right on His face.

• • •

When you need to set boundaries . . .

> *They are the kind [of people] who work*
> *their way into people's homes and win the*
> *confidence of vulnerable women who are*
> *burdened with the guilt of sin and con-*
> *trolled by various desires.*
>
> 2 TIMOTHY 3:6

THE POWER TO choose is so inherently God-given that Scripture raises a gigantic red flag over people who make us feel so weak we can't make a sound decision.

I totally resonate with Paul's warning to Timothy. A person cannot be whole in a relationship where he or she feels powerless to make healthy choices.

• • •

*We will speak the truth in love, growing in
every way more and more like Christ, who
is the head of his body, the church.*

EPHESIANS 4:15

CONFRONTING SOMEONE IS hard, and the risk of
discovering something worse than you suspect can
be enough to paralyze you until the whole relationship goes up in smoke.

The alternative to practicing what Scripture
calls speaking the truth in love is continuing to
communicate a lie in fear. That's no way to live.

• • •

When you are searching for an identity . . .

> *Don't be misled, my dear brothers and sisters. Whatever is good and perfect comes down to us from God our Father, who created all the lights in the heavens. He never changes or casts a shifting shadow. He chose to give birth to us by giving us his true word. And we, out of all creation, became his prized possession.*
>
> JAMES 1:16-18

IDENTITY AS THE introduction to intimacy is the whole idea behind God telling Moses in Exodus 33 that He knew him by name. The same was true when Christ called Himself the Good Shepherd in John 10 and told His disciples that "he calls his own sheep *by name*" (emphasis added).

• • •

Jesus began a tour of the nearby towns and villages, preaching and announcing the Good News about the Kingdom of God. He took his twelve disciples with him, along with some women who had been cured of evil spirits and diseases.　LUKE 8:1-2

IN A CULTURE where some sects of Pharisees started their day by thanking God they were not born a woman, Jesus had a passel of women right at His side.

To be called is a wondrous thing indeed. In fact, that very word is used in reference to the way every Christian, regardless of gender, first comes to Christ (Romans 8:30). But here in this portion of Luke's eloquent Gospel, alongside "the Twelve" were also "some women who had been cured." I know the feeling.

• • •

When you are feeling unlovable . . .

The LORD says, "Then I will heal you of
your unfaithfulness; my love will know no
bounds, for my anger will be gone forever."

HOSEA 14:4

THAT'S WHAT HAPPENED to me. God cured me of
my own gross unfaithfulness. He healed my unlove-
liness with His own love. As I live and breathe, I
am not the woman I used to be.

• • •

How lovely is your dwelling place, O LORD
of Heaven's Armies. PSALM 84:1

I MEMORIZED THAT wonderful pilgrim psalm many years ago, but not once have I ever seen the opening verse in light of believers as the current dwelling places of God's Spirit. Imagine how different our days would be if we woke up every morning and, before putting on a stitch of makeup or flat-ironing our hair, we confessed out loud to God: "How lovely is your dwelling place, O Lord of Heaven's Armies!"

•••

Let all that I am praise the LORD; with my whole heart, I will praise his holy name. Let all that I am praise the LORD; may I never forget the good things he does for me. He forgives all my sins and heals all my diseases.

PSALM 103:1-3

THE PSALMIST LIKELY didn't command his soul to praise because that's what he felt like doing anyway. I believe he caught himself in the act of destructive or distracted thinking and intended to change the course of his thoughts. That's exactly what you and I must do if we want to start living like the secure

people God created us to be. We must catch ourselves in the act of unhealthy thinking and call our
souls to switch tracks.

• • •

When you are tired of competition and conflict . . .

> *Since we are living by the Spirit, let us*
> *follow the Spirit's leading in every part of*
> *our lives. Let us not become conceited, or*
> *provoke one another, or be jealous of one*
> *another.* GALATIANS 5:25-26

THESE ARE SOME great words straight off the sacred page that we can use to whisper to ourselves when we're tempted to enter the competition our culture has cast between women.

• • •

> *Don't repay evil for evil. Don't retaliate*
> *with insults when people insult you. Instead,*

pay them back with a blessing. That is what
God has called you to do, and he will bless
you for it.   I PETER 3:9

I KEEP THIS verse in the recesses of my mind so I
can recall how God can work in a harsh conflict.
It's how we take the high road when somebody is
begging us to mud wrestle with her in the potholes
of the low road.

● ● ●

When you need Christ's saving power . . .

No, this is the kind of fasting I want: Free those who are wrongly imprisoned; lighten the burden of those who work for you. Let the oppressed go free, and remove the chains that bind people. Share your food with the hungry, and give shelter to the homeless. Give clothes to those who need them, and do not hide from relatives who need your help. Then your salvation will come like the dawn, and your wounds will quickly heal. Your godliness will lead you forward, and the glory of the LORD will protect you from behind. Then when you call, the LORD will answer. "Yes, I am here," he will quickly

reply. Remove the heavy yoke of oppression.
Stop pointing your finger and spreading
vicious rumors! Feed the hungry, and help
those in trouble. Then your light will shine
out from the darkness, and the darkness
around you will be as bright as noon. The
LORD will guide you continually, giving you
water when you are dry and restoring your
strength. You will be like a well-watered
garden, like an ever-flowing spring.

ISAIAH 58:6-11

ONE OF MY worst nightmares was that in trying to do the right thing, I would shape our children's theologies in such a way that they would see God as the Big Taker in the Sky instead of the Giver of "every good and perfect gift" (James 1:17, NIV). I never wanted them to think that the only word He had uttered since the conclusion of the sacred canon was no.

• • •

He will be your sure foundation, provid-
ing a rich store of salvation, wisdom, and

> *knowledge. The fear of the LORD will be*
> *your treasure.*   ISAIAH 33:6

TRUST GOD.

Plain and simple. Not easy, mind you, but basic and uncomplicated. You don't always have to hash it all out. Sometimes you can make a single swift decision. As Christ said to a wavering disciple, you just have to make up your splintered mind to "stop doubting and believe" (John 20:27, NIV). Believe that He loves you and has you covered and takes every one of your hits as if they were aimed at His own skin. Get down to the bottom of what frightens you, and then pitch it to Him like a hot potato.

If we can't count on God, for crying out loud, who can we count on?

• • •

> *Trust in the LORD with all your heart; do*
> *not depend on your own understanding.*
> *Seek his will in all you do, and he will show*
> *you which path to take.*
>
>   PROVERBS 3:5-6

FOR TIMES WHEN action is necessary but not obvious, Solomon hits the nail on the head in this passage. Trust God.

• • •

The LORD is your security. He will keep
your foot from being caught in a trap.

PROVERBS 3:26

TAKE YOUR DIGNITY back no matter where you've been or what has happened to you. Hold on to your security for all you're worth. It is yours. Nothing and no one can take it from you.

• • •

"The message is very close at hand; it is
on your lips and in your heart." And that
message is the very message about faith that
we preach: If you confess with your mouth
that Jesus is Lord and believe in your heart
that God raised him from the dead, you will
be saved. For it is by believing in your heart
that you are made right with God, and it
is by confessing with your mouth that you

are saved. As the Scriptures tell us, "Anyone who trusts in him will never be disgraced." Jew and Gentile are the same in this respect. They have the same Lord, who gives generously to all who call on him. For "Everyone who calls on the name of the LORD will be saved." ROMANS 10:8-13

I COULD HAVE no greater privilege in all of life than introducing you to a saving relationship with Jesus Christ. You will realize as time goes on that no human being could draw you here. This invitation is from Christ alone. He has been pursuing you for years, and now if you are willing and so desire, the time has come to start living the life you were created for. The simplicity of the gospel is often a stumbling block for people. We reason that eternal life in heaven and internal power on earth should take longer to acquire than five minutes, but that's where we misunderstand who is doing the work.

Jesus already spent the time, energy, and unimaginable turmoil when He went to the cross. All you're asked to do is receive the gift He has placed with unbridled affection before you. Once you've accepted

His gift of grace, you don't need to ever doubt your salvation again. Your eternal condition is not based on how you feel from day to day. Stand steadfastly on what you know. The very moment you accept Christ as your Savior, you receive His Spirit. Once He resides within you, He will never leave or forsake you. When you die, you will awaken immediately to brand-new life in a glorious Kingdom, where you will be more alive than you ever dreamed of being on earth. Let this matter be settled once and for all. Know that nothing and no one, including you, can sabotage your salvation.

• • •

Your journey doesn't end when you finish this book.

Dig deeper
into this important topic with Beth and other women as
they continue to discuss *So Long, Insecurity* on her blog at
livingproofministries.blogspot.com.

CP0363